PS.ARCHIVE

Vol-1

For all my beloved muses

RARITY
ETHEREAL HOME
VIOLIN'S STRING
EUGENE
ROUSE OF CHAPTER NO.2
IN SEARCH OF HUE, YOU
—

MINE AND MYSELF

I'M NOT URBAN

Sunrises and morning walks

Paddy fields and bullock carts

It was a cheap shot that I'm not an urban.

Cold shoulders to slander talks

Never tried to hit the marts

It was a cheap shot that I'm not an urban.

They declare, "She could never play a full deck."

Always treated like an ape, I wrecked

Jump on the bandwagon; lost minds want the world's pick

Crowded cobblestones make me sick

Their rack and pinion

Loading my neck and head

It was a cheap shot that I'm not an urban.

Shrewd sacks of opinion,

But I see nothing ahead.

It was a cheap shot that I'm not an urban.

They assured me, "Waste not, want not, work for a paycheck."

That made me feel the choke at the tip of a bottleneck.
I'm pure undisturbed gold, not a pinchbeck.
I learned the hard way. I trek.

To settle down and be governed was all they needed.
Until I bowed and broiled, they all kneaded.

From weddings to funerals, they blathered till I withered
In temples and sanctuaries, I saw how peace fled
From peer to stranger, everyone wants to dust my bed
It was their cheap shot that I'm not an urban.

They failed to realize that I was dog-tired
By the burning questions that was fired
Solitude was all I required,
Because, I lost myself, being tangled and wired.
To be someone, I always aspired
But to do something, I was never inspired.
With all my words, I shed red
Knowing you are all I ever desired.

To give up on all their talk, I was certain
It was their cheap shot that I'm not an urban.

AIN'T A HUFFLEPUFF

This is what healing feels like
Earth laughs through flowers alike.
Sitting under the navy blue sky
It makes me want to fly.

Trees dancing to my beat
Like a break from all the heat.
Breeze waft like never before
Like God's hug, I'm feeling secure.

Distress and repose; hike
Nothing feels soothing, unlike
Tears are arrested at the edge of my eye.
Should it be this way? Why?

Life necessitates affirmation
"You are doing well enough."
Dwelling in a puddle of emotion,
And trying to feel nothing is tough.
Do I not deserve comprehension?
I guess I waited long enough.
"I'm happy", my deadly delusion

I ain't a hufflepuff.

Tormented under the burning sun
Regrets weighed a million tons.
I'm not used to soft, subtle breeze
I can never be at ease.

Qualm grew over the feeling of being loved
Bereaved, the fear in me grew.
To God, with faith, I bowed
Instant proof that it isn't true.

It was sickening,
Bedlam is buzzing like bees.
This instance is an awakening,
"The truth will set you free."

I repel confrontation
Otherwise, times get rough.
Left with no agitation
I learnt I'm never out of delusion
"I'm happy"; I chose to bluff.
Antonym of perfection
I ain't a hufflepuff.

I look forward to seeing you in anticipation.
I've had much more than enough.
To go ahead, there's hesitation
I feel like I'm under a tight cuff.
I worked with dedication
But I can't take another rebuff.
Queen of affection
Still ain't a hufflepuff.

HAD IT ALL

A team of fifteen met when we were nineteen
Bonded as family, though we were quarantined.
A year ago, we started off as just nine
The girls have passed out, and the guys didn't touch the wine.
Running late to classes, heart and eyes pounding
Crossed all the leaps, unbreakable bonding
Spilling tea, our days, and our coffees
Never bothered to exchange birthday toffees

We did nothing great but just walked through a mall
We can't afford to attend a fancy prom ball.
Fear of the future, from within, a scary crawl
But by just being there, we almost had it all.

Caught off guard, losing the phone to the dean
We totally can't handle girls who are mean.
Troop of crackheads, blunder in design
Screaming at movies, getting chills in the spine.
Marching proudly, classes absconding
So rightfully, as if we own the building
Teasing and laughing, we easily make a scene.
Hands down, we work hard and are very keen.

We did nothing great but just walked through a mall.
We can't afford to attend a fancy prom ball.
Fear of the future, from within, a scary crawl
But by just being there, we almost had it all.

TALE OF SCARS

I'm dressed in all white
Under warm daylight.
It's always been in my head
It's never been alright.

Just a couple of years ago
Wild troops, I happen to know
Winter snow, said our first hello.
Till now we managed to balance in one toe

All the tales of scars have just faded away
I never fit the game; I didn't want to stay.
I have nothing more to say
My vision is gray, locked in a bay.

False taste of delight
Like downfall from a flight
I never dared to die
Still lurching on the edge of a height

Learning my boundaries
At ease, as ladies

Never as perfect as movies
So I got hurt in an ordered series.

All the tales of scars started in May.
All the words I say were always cliche.
Every other Friday
I felt like a homeless stray.

All the tales of scars never fade away.
I find a new way every single day.
On the grass, I lay
Unbothered about my pay

AM I?

Who am I, really?

It's past midnight.

I couldn't sleep.

I cry, and I really want to die.

Dared to dive from a height

Into the deep dark

Who am I, really?

Am I a goddess or am I modest?

Am I a worthy heir or a mother?

Am I a burden to this world?

These thoughts are tightly nailed

A dawn without me will still be bright.

I'm serving no point.

And I ain't a knight.

Weary, my eyes teary

At eternal gnaw

I have no color palette.

Clearly, only in theory

I fight the claw.

In a real, an inert piglet!

Am I intense? Am I zealous?
Am I a lover or a suitor?
Through all the thin and thin
I've been all alone.

A dawn without me will still be bright.
I'm serving no point.
And I ain't a knight.

KING AND KINGDOM

THE KING

Once, Little Verena lived in a huge castle.
Feeling caged and lonely, plucking basil
Wanting to live up to her own dreams, terms, and conditions
She grew up with the ideologies of the king
The only setback was the idea of a ring.

In exile to a barren land filled with sonder
The king appointed a comply with an archer.
Presuming herself to be the prey,
She concealed herself under the wedges.
It took a long time for her to realize
It was so sedative that it was after the king's demise.

The shoulder-high villainic archer walked her way to the crown.
Shredding and grasping the fanatic love of the two with a frown.
She starts her reign with the principles of the king.
On the dais, where the archer has always gazed at the king
Now I guess he is proud of his little Varena being a decorated queen.

THE GOLDFISH POOL

Home ain't home anymore

He walks in the hallway, like the King Lion's deep roar

Her jewels are still there, in a keyless royal drawer

I could still see him

I could still see her on the swing, dressed up and prim

Down right woe grief

Slithered my only possession, nature is an evil thief.

In the cold weather, that's when they glide like an old elm leaf.

Bereft rough pour

Home ain't home anymore

The littoral seemed bright, blue, and beautiful.

Loved ones only grasp the taste; it's cruel.

I could only plead with God to change the rule

Devils are laughing from under the goldfish pool.

In all my flashbacks, I wish there was at least some candor

I walked in thorny shoes, yet regrets are on the floor.

Foolishly, hopefully, I will keep looking through the door.

What else could I do with memories but store?

Home ain’t home anymore.
I can't take the fact that they are no more.
Looking back, all the stills and frames feel sour.
I really miss them.
Acceptance is a layer over living memories like skim

Down right woe grief
I stand there and cry at the midsea reef.
Men may come and go, but they'll be my forever chiefs.
I bawl from my core.
Home ain’t home anymore.

The littoral seemed bright, blue, and beautiful
Loved ones only grasp the taste; demise is cruel.
I could only plead with God to change the rule
Devils are laughing from under the goldfish pool.

Anytime I look back, I wish there was at least candor
I walked in thorny shoes, yet regrets are on the floor.
Foolishly, hopefully, I will keep waiting at the door
What else could I do with memories but store?

O' DEAR LORD

Mourning and grieving
The eyes keep tearing.
My heart is aching.
Pond belt, facing
I end up losing.

Every morning, a very fresh greeting
Out of rhythm, how did we both sing?
O' dear lord, O' dear lord
It is a sudden stop of breezing.
I was out of breath. I, too, ended up breathing.

Only man I've ever bowed to. He was the king.
Now I'm all alone in the castle swing.
O' dear lord, O' dear lord
There was a sudden stop of pouring.
I would be a drought land without his homecoming.

The moment I saw the coffin coming
Further, nevermore, that was my feeling.
O' dear lord, O' dear lord
Why should there always be an ending?

He was my route, and now I'm becoming

A girl in midsea, his hand I was leaving
Through the moonglade, I'm walking.
O' dear lord, O' dear lord
To make him proud, I'm striving,
To be sound and sane after his passing

Mourning and grieving
Eyes keep tearing.
My heart is aching.
Pond belt, facing
I end up losing.

KING AGAIN

I wish I hugged just a little more.
A little more; I should've talked
Talked to him and cried.

Cried and dead, I'm standing right there.
Right there, where he left me
Left me and flew away from my life.

Life is ill-lit without him.
Without him, everything would be so still.
Still flame; truly, I am.
I am unable to enlighten
Enlighten myself as a whole.

As a whole, he was my only home.
Home, where he will never be back
Back to the days when we opened a sweet can
Can he ever be the king again?

Again, the greed era
Era that he buried fifteen years ago
Ago is much like in the past.

Past, when they stabbed his back.
Back then, when everything was settled
Settled but not solved
Solved by karma, they paid their whole lives.

Life is ill-lit without him.
Without him, everything would be so still
Still flame; truly, I am.
I am unable to enlighten
Enlighten myself as a whole.

As a whole, he was my only home.
Home, where he will never be back
Back to the days when we opened a sweet can
Can he ever be the King again?

Again, from the beginning, they were scheming.
Scheming for the throne
The throne that didn't make him the regal king of the state.
The state that was and will be ruled by the legacy of his life.

Life is ill-lit without him.
Without him, everything would be so still
Still flame; truly, I am.

I am unable to enlighten

Enlighten myself as a whole.

As a whole, he was my only home.

Home, where he will never be back

Back to the days when we opened a sweet can

Can he ever be the King again?

DRAINING TIME

I stopped wearing watches

In my sinister hand.

The regret in me hatches

Grief that I can't stand.

I dropped my cloche

The truth went in the sand.

At the edge of the notch

Sundial time, is all we had.

The fragrance of his room, where we talked all night

"There is never another time", surged in plight.

I thought I could accept his absence all these days.

And I keep singing his glory and praise.

I know that he is gone.

And the time we had will never be born.

Gathering it all

It makes me bawl.

I stood there awhile in our backyard garden rain.

Thinking of our time together, I blue-blooded my veins.

Holding the dime one more time

I had a breakdown in my spine.

I served his favorites on his dinner plate
Complaining about how much food he threw in the waste.
We watched a historical fiction film for five hours straight
Till the very end, we didn't get the characters right.

Every other day, bedtime
We argued over vine.
I always want you around
Now I'm dead and drowned.
Every other morning walks
With crofters, his small talks.
I gave a side stare,
Too bored to speak fair.

Till the hourglass sand was drained
And when my arms and legs were chained.
Till when I went insane
In irresistible pain.
Only with him was I contained
To him, my life was completely ingrained.

It was too soon for him
To leave me alone at dim.

I accepted it right away
But I keep crying every single day.

I stood there awhile in his drawing room
Clueless and quiet, like a baby in the womb.
Holding the dime one more time
I had a breakdown in my spine.

I stood there awhile, where no one cared to see
In my efforts to jump into the deep blue sea.
Holding the dime one more time
I had a breakdown in my spine.

He was my one and only strength,
My one and only love.
I knew this day would surely come
But I never thought of what I would become.
He was mine, gone in no time
I had a breakdown in my spine.

For his return home
I wait like a loon.
My wait never ended
And will never end.

The hands of his watch stiffen.
Who'll ever join me for wine?
I had a breakdown in my spine.

"Time and love can't be bought with money."
I'm standing here alone, in complete agony.
Losing both, I realized the maturescence with age
I got the courage to walk out of the cage.

I named myself after his dear mother.
To say, "You are my chief, and there's no other."
I'm wearing his watch; it's now mine.
I'm now used to the breakdown in my spine.

I stood there a while, in front of the whole world
Trying to prove that I am strong-willed.
Acclaiming the time, one more time
I feel a breakdown in my spine.
Lying, I'm fine, one more time,
I had a breakdown in my spine.
Holding the dime one more time
I had a breakdown in my spine.

And all the wisest men in the world

Sure-shot claim

That the skin's memory is just three months time

I just realized I forgot your touch.

That thought in me wildly grows like a blue grutch.

DIE ____ DIGNITY

Will I ever come through?
No one feels as deeply as I do.
I stood against an old mirror.
Wondering if they can't come any nearer.

This feeling grows in me, thick.
Like a train journey without music
"Time and tide wait for none."
Quietly, they're gone.

"Die for dignity."
She did with humility.
"Die with dignity"
He lived like royalty.
Slept in serenity,
They knew it was meant for the nobility.
"Die for dignity."
"Die with dignity"

The greedy got what they wanted.
They had all of this plotted.
Their screams and games didn't go in vain.

They acted like pure, evil saints.

Sixty years of togetherness
They fed even the rotten ones.
It was a blunder that they did hesitate.
And they never fumigate.

"Die for dignity."
She did with humility.
"Die with dignity"
He lived like royalty.
Their ecstasy, feeding the snake community
That was their lenity.
"Die for dignity."
"Die with dignity"

I can't have faith anymore.
I've had enough. But I want more.
I waited, gazing through the front door.
Tears decorate the bloody floor.
What is all this for?
They always swore

"Die for dignity."

She did with humility.

“Die with dignity”

He lived like royalty.

Silver bar priority: relationships are salty.

Still, it is our ethnicity.

“Die for dignity.”

“Die with dignity”

CLAIR DE LUNE

YOU SAID IT ONCE

I cried on my birthday,
Being called "a sinful bane"
Not being enough for myself and my loved ones
Having no great flair
Too fast to fit in anywhere
Now I'm done with everyone all at once.

"Find your name, find yourself."
"Sky always gives you a reason to live."
You said it once; you said it all once.
It's you and nothing else.
The love that you could only give
Liberate me from sins; liberate me from all my sins.

The sky is filled with stars.
I'm seeing the universe from afar.
From behind the illusory bars
From behind the unreal spars

This blue never fades.
Never fades into a lighter shade
Crushing me for decades

Planting me under the blades

"It's still worth living."
"Fall in love with being alive."
You said it once; you said it all once.
I keep misgiving.
Still I thrive to survive.
Liberate me from sins; liberate me from all my sins.

From my lily garden,
I couldn't unearth you.
My love isn't sudden
You were always my hue.
I am smitten
By your beautiful blue.

"We win some and lose some."
"We'll let moonlight guide us."
You said it once; you said it all once.
I'll try not to succumb.
I'll try not to rust.
Liberate me from sins; liberate me from all my sins.

HIRAETH

It was extreme, hard-core agony.
I wish you had been here, dear honey.
Fake laughing at all the silly plots,
My dreams and life suddenly halts

I think I don't fit in anywhere anymore.
Except for your wide, open arm
The feeling that you'll be my forever home
The hiraeth that's always along
I've been trying so hard.
To give up and walk ahead

Will you ever come and bail me?
I'm always at stake, and I'm sorry.
I killed them, and my hands are bloody.

Lost the soul taste of happiness
I could've never cried a little less.
Maroon cushion, dug my head, and pressed

I think I don't fit in anywhere anymore.
Except for your wide, open arm

The feeling that you'll be my forever home
The hiraeth that's always along
I've been trying so hard.
To give up and walk ahead

I want to cut myself into two halves.
Or run away, to a place far away.
I was never brave enough to do it.
But to find you, I had all the grit.

What I wanted all this time
Is us aging like fine wine.
I'm roaming all alone.
Please be my forever home.

I think I don't fit in anywhere anymore.
Except for your wide, open arm
The feeling that you'll be my forever home
And the hiraeth that's always along
I've been trying so hard.
To give up and walk ahead

I could never walk ahead.
You are my forever home.

SOMEDAY OR ANOTHER

Hand-inked love letters
To dimple smile and dragon, brown eyes
I forbear the anguish pang.
Trivia love, from another state
Thinking "now" is never too late.
I forbear the anguish pang.

I see you speaking words of wisdom,
Talking coherently in rhythm
I see you entering the White House.
For our terrain's rise and rouse
All I want is nothing more than us being together.
I hope it comes true some day or another.

A sidekick for everyone
My meaning of love is that you are the one.
It's my conviction that keeps me pushing.

I see us. Find our lovely home,
Wherever we roam
I see us holding hands,
And walking through the street ends.

All I want is nothing more than us being together.
I hope it comes true some day or another.

My expedition to reach you is never-ending.
All my life, to love you, I've been viking.

'Cause “we are destined to be”, says the moonphase.
Then on, we’ll be perfect, like a never-ending kiss.
Altered me endlessly, your indigo trace
Someday or another, there will be an end to my chase.

On a rainy day, I see us moving for Frederic
I’m with you inside your turtleneck.
In that warmth, you leave a subtle peck.
I know I can’t make a horse drink.
But I believe in fate, fortune, and luck.
Besides you, all the gold and silver is seck.
I hope I’m the one sealed off from the deck.
Off your company, I totally wreck

All I want is nothing more than us being together.
I hope it comes true some day or another.

ENDEARED OR ENDURED

I’ve never belonged, but I'm just staying.
Fate always failed me, aimless straying
I wish I had fled and never shown back.
My brightness had a dear slack.

I gazed at the sky and never caught the rainbow.
Forever I bided by the window.
“Home is a person”, I never knew.
I invariably waited for something new.

First girl, plainly treated special
It takes forever to find my potential.
Scared of stepping out of the shade
I’m sure my traces will fade.

I’m on a hamster wheel. I try to shear.
My morale signs shouldn’t disappear.
I presumed I was born to be endeared.
But for some reason, I feel endured.

Loving any person when they leave
And acceding when I had to proceed

Settling for less and wanting more

You, my moonshot, are my life lore.

It feels like you are near.

My impressions are singular and austere.

I presumed I was born to be endeared.

But for some reason, I felt endured.

THROUGH BLACK AND BLUE

"I lived like a lark"
That was my pea-brained illusion.
Waiting for the spark
To decipher my ambition

One of the rarest species
Opinions are treated like royal feces.
A boundless haul
To cross over the morale wall

It's the biggest hurdle.
I'm pure milk, off to curdle.
My heart's got a slit.
To prove it

I ain't a twit,
Or a dumb role in the skit
My eyes grew dewy.
Through black and blue
At this pace,
There's no end to my chase.
My certitude flew

Through black and blue

No thick bark
That was my only definition.
I've been very stark.
My abyss needs more conception.

There's no clear theses.
In the little old valise
At times, there's a squall.
To face it, I've thrall

Feeling tiny and little
Reared well to clean spittle
There is nothing wrong with doing it.
Until it hurts the heart

I don't worry a bit.
To jump into your pit
'Cause it has been you.
Through black and blue
To walk out of the race
To cry with grace
Take me through.

Through black and blue

Feeling only for you
Through black and blue
Who could give me hue?
Through black and blue

To do a good thing
Only you, I'm counting
To do so, the bad thing
Only you; I'm hunting.
To live through everything
With only you, I'm fighting.

I learned not to fit
But to build a fort.
To come to you
Through black and blue
Just in case
If I stormed your space
I deeply regret
Through black and blue

To do a good thing

Through black and blue

To do so, the bad thing

Through black and blue

To live through everything

Through black and blue

WILL WE EVER BE REAL?

The whole world brightens in your astral aglow.
It follows your rhythm, wades, and grows.
I've loved you since ages ago—years in a row.
I've loved you so

In the darkest, dim, and dingy night
Life glitzes and lusters your light.
In times of tough fighting, hold on tight
To radiate lives bright.

Every day, I die and burn into ashes with zeal.
Will we both ever be real?

I'll be your sun.
You are my moon.
We are day and night. That'll never combine.
Nature never lets us intertwine.
I waited all my life.
Choking in the strife
Someday, destiny will bring us together.
I will fly to you like a feather.

"When you're about to forget, I'll be right back."
I'm getting down. It's already dusk.
I acted all brisk, but I'm about to break.
Honey, I'm at stake.
You're my savior, my dear armor.
The missing color, you'll be my lover.
Even if it's a mistake, it's my take.
Honey, I won't forsake

Every day, without you, day and night, the same wheel
Will we both ever be real?

I'll be your sun.
You are my moon.
We are day and night. That'll never combine.
Nature never lets us intertwine.
I waited all my life.
Choking in the strife
Someday, destiny will bring us together.
I will fly to you like a feather.

When it's dawn now, the time when you and I show up
I would very much want to lock it all up.

I’ll be your sun.

You are my moon.

We’re the rarest treasures of nature.

I pray your service is safer.

I’ll wait all my life.

Even under a sharp-edged knife

For you to be my forever home

Nothing more than just you alone

HOPELESSLY IN LOVE

We could be two people from very different roots.
But why do I feel like we'll pull it off?
Like the gleaming Venus beside the full moon
I just want to be by your side forever.

I realize I'm hopelessly in love.
It's getting intense; I don't know how.
In his grace, who is up above
Dressed like a dove, to say the vow
The real classic ring on my glove
It says it all: I'm hopelessly in love.

We could be two people with different tongues.
But our words speak our hearts out.
Having our own visions for the time ahead
We shall share our future forever.

We shall stand at the altar holding hands
Till death do us part, till blue on our faces
Till the very end of time and chime
Do be my forever
We shall create our world with no end

In sickness and health, we both swear
For rich and poor, from mansion to shack
I'll be your forever

I realize I'm hopelessly in love.
It's getting intense; I don't know how.
In his grace, who is up above
Dressed like a dove, to say the vow
The real classic ring on my glove
It says it all: I'm hopelessly in love.

ONLY YOU

Call me an old soul.

Native, a rabbit hole

Gazing at red sunsets

Leaning back, breezes

Sadness and poetry

Solicit solitary

Just an ordinary girl

Honor and glory

Carry my story.

Climb to you,my love

Don't ask me how.

I should be deserving.

For that, I'm striving

By tossing a pearl.

You are up there, on the center stage.

I have loved you since the Holocene age.

I have odds to fight with rage.

You are the words on my page.

When I give up and think, "Come soon,"

Nature acknowledges, “He is your moon.”
“Around the time when you’re beginning to forget.”
“I’ll come and find you”, his fortuitous offset

It’s destiny; we can’t walk past it.
Your subtle smile fades all the somber and slit
I don’t want anyone but you.
Whenever I’m lost, you are my cue.

Hundredth time, I’m losing
Yet, you, I’m choosing
I fall only deep
Where no one could sweep.
Head over heels
My tough skin peels.
I ain’t fragile.

Touching the wrong nerves
That’s love from Ivy Servers.
I’m in distress
Tearing my dress.
I’ll not care a bit
When I make it.
I’ll walk down the aisle.

You are up there, in the spotlight.
I can't touch it; it's shining bright.
Time without you, I fear
Soaken pages, you are my tear.

I might be expecting
You could be neglecting.
I'm not your acquaintance
Handle me with some patience.
It has been a long while
How do I dial?
To learn behind the mask
I know it's too much to ask.

But when I stumble and think, "Come soon,"
Nature acknowledges, "He is your moon."
"Around the time when you're beginning to forget."
"I'll come and find you", your fortuitous offset

It's destiny; we can't walk past it.
Your subtle smile fades all the somber and slit
I don't want anyone but you.
You are the light in my life and hue.

WILL YOU CROSS THE LINE?

Thick and thin
Through thick and thin
Through the rain and shine
Through whiskey and wine
Through all the pleasure and pain
Be my Valentine,
And cross the line.
Will you cross the line?

Body and mind
Between body and mind
I couldn't find
Where I'm left behind
And to see love, I'm blind.
Shall we be intertwined,
And cross the line?
Will you cross the line?

Don't ask me why.
Why can't I go past this line?
To come to you, a true defy
My love is unsaid, unrequited, and divine.

Still cross the line.

Will you cross the line?

I will come.

Across oceans

Across cliffs

Across valleys

In love

I will come.

Across countries

Across borders, across atlases

But it is indifferent for the sun to show up at night.

So will you cross the line?

I'm sorry

I'm too much; I'm sorry.

This love, I can't burry

Our life together will be merry,

Having great chemistry

We shall be legendary.

So, cross the line.

Will you cross the line?

I waited a while.

For nature to play its game

Life keeps going, a hightail

All this time, I chanted your name.

Did I cross the line?

If not, will you cross the line?

I'm fighting

Against reality

Against values

Against virtues

In love

I'm fighting

Inability, actuality

Losing sanity

I'm on the edge; I can't take a step forward.

So, will you cross the line?

I've come a little too far.

Saying, "All is fair in love and war."

But now I'm crying shame.

Counting all my words that are lame

Now, will you cross the line?

Will you cross the line?

At all times

When I cry

When I smile

When I scowl

In love

With true faith

I'm waiting, craving

And hoping

For us to be an actual thing

Will you cross the line?

Love my warts and all.

Even when I fall

If I don't recall

Stab me with an awl.

Do you hear my howl?

For love, I prowl.

Between fair play and foul

Will you ever cross the line?

THANKS FOR LOVE?

ATLAS

Compact inn lodge

He walked into the lounge.

To pick up a crowd

Drive down town road

Street lights, in and out

Entrance, he did scout.

Snugged for a long time

Homelike wed dine

Debut and small talk

Swift by crosswalk

Playlist handed in

His mum was calling.

The next day, same car

Outside ice cream bar

I waved a huge hi!

Across the road, he stood by.

When he dropped us and gave me his hand

The girls were his fans. Why I understand

Maroon and beige cushions made me retent

I totally loved his extreme kind end.

And on that night, the native slang that he used,

Made me stupor and think that "this is a prelude."
That's when I realized what it feels like in real.
But there is a halt; he knew it all.

He reached back twice.
The tough parts were byes.
Soda as breakfast
Coffee on insist
"Thanks for your love."
I went a step above.
Called him, broken voice.
That was the best choice.
He dressed in a dapper
I, drenched in rainwater
Ate ice cream bites
And we played word games.
12 feet gap, I walk
Royals like small talk.
Flavored drink jug
The goodbye hug

I closed my eyes and held back a tiny tear.
I pushed myself to the verge of mild despair.
I broke off the hug and took in the fact

That I totally loved his extreme, kind end.

He softly and gently made me realize

Not every puzzle piece will fit "Precise."

Three days I bawled, the dramatic phone call.

But there is a halt; I knew it all.

In all the midnight deep blue still sea silences

He never made me feel like I was pushing beyond my bounds.

All I ever wanted was to be someone he remembered.

But I still wonder how someone could enkindle such warmth.

I loved his extreme, kind end.

But there is always an end.

SOFT BREEZE

It took a whole lunar phase for me to realize
"Everything is just what I fantasize."
It was too soon for me to think about any of these.
I couldn't help; he was a soft breeze.

It just felt like home, but I can't stay forever and ever and ever.
Yet I can walk down, happy or sad, whenever and however

All the wisdom he imparted from his past
Well-taught me to "have no hope" until the very last
It was too soon for me to think about all these
I couldn't help; he was a soft breeze.

On and off, vibrant and loud, on a dead-end road
Waves hit the shore, touching me like never before.
Still, scary, deep, quiet, and very personal from within.
Where the divers and dolphins can never swoop in

I whelve on the shore, sad and hard to stand again and again.
"I want to be Venus beside the golden shining moon", I exclaim.

I knew waves don't stay.

I'll return to this shore with true contentment to look at the future I gave away

Until then,

Keep it all in, the sorrow and misery I cried out.

Keep it all in, the inside jokes I can't laugh at.

Keep it all in, the memories I built from miles afar.

Soft breeze, please keep it all in

OATH OF GOD

Betty, from a silent village
With a very well-set image
Being the headman's daughter
Hates being around water
Been constantly gawked
Gold ring, set to be hawked
She spent her days alive and quiet.
Under midday white sunlight
Anything off for Kin?
Or disrepair is a sin.
It was her lavish rage.
To break the golden cage
Monotonous and dull
Yet loud and communal
Safety and interests
Never let her see sunsets.

One fine evening, she met a prince of a 'city by the sea'.
Vibrant and colorful, red sky and sunsets, she asked to see
The boat got off the shore. He said, "Carpe diem, why not?"
She wore a candid smile and thought, "Maybe this is the spot."

Hear the loud crowd cheer.

Can't fit in, her genuine fear

Ready to duly walk out

From the dream, she snaps out

Goodbye letter and an umbrella

She learned Eric didn't kill Ursula.

Lost in her dull thoughts

She untied all the knots.

Slowly, the sun goes down.

She felt better than a clown.

It was all in her head.

This was his only dread.

That she might cast hope

Trying too hard to cope

Then Rayleigh Red

That's when she said

"I don't know if it's right for me to say this, but I'll miss you."

She realized that no light flooded her retina with any hue.

It took her light years and tight lessons to walk back to the shore.

She stood there, remembering times with her fore

Her eyes were dewy for the first time, looking at the midnight sky.

All the unreasonable, pointless dots made sense for once.

Unbearable loss of the one man she ever loved, the King

That's the Oath of God.

The burning light that she had practiced was of no use.

From the shore, she walked down the moonglade towards her moon.

The still sea set by the prince paved her way to be Venus.

That's the Oath of God.

HEART OF THE OCEAN

Sudden, nice weather

Amidst a hot, burning summer

Soft breeze cooling

Hinted at his homecoming.

It took a lot of effort.

And real long days

To build back grace

The tiebreaker between heart and mind

I don't remember if it was rightly chosen.

He was candid, casual, and cool as the wind.

I do know why. I threw the Heart of the Ocean

I still stood there.

Close to the offshore bar

To take a handful of sand

As a souvenir to my land

Passion measurement

Exiled enchantment

I can't tell "rightly credited."

The tiebreaker between heart and mind

I don't remember if it was rightly chosen.
I am color blind, and I am one of a kind.
I do know why. I threw the heart of the ocean.

When the waves bring it back to me
Beneath my feet, from the deep sea
In a bowl, wild fish quell pain.
My blood congealed in my veins.

I'm not the one to get it.
I know the value of it.
Still not entailing it.
It was never mine.
And it would never be mine

The tiebreaker between heart and mind
I don't remember if it was rightly chosen.
He's team English; my patriotism is tested.
I do know why. I gave up on the only hope diamond.
I do know why. I lost it because it was brutally cursed.
I do know why. I threw the Heart of the Ocean

INDIGO REVERI_

INDIGO REVERIE

They are my amateur words, honey.
Will that fetch me some money?
I have no idea what to do next.
You are my **indigo** reverie.
I'm not good enough. I'm sorry
I've tried my best.

The raging urge to console characters
Or cry with them all the way down,
In every other poignant picture.
Wherever I feel, their pain is what I own.
"When it rains, it pours."
This long wait is sour.

Mornings aren't anymore lovely.
Jokes aren't anymore funny.
Is it difficult because it's the last test?
You are my indigo reverie,
Whose love would set me free?
Because of that, there should be a glimpse first.

I realized I was incomplete in all the chapters.

Like a torn, burning gown
My body is filled with incurable blisters.
Still, faith is deeply sown.
I've always wanted more.
So I escaped through the back door.

I'll escape with a heavy cape.
Will I survive? 'cause I can't revive.
And that's it; I'm walking out.
Will you ever come and scout?
I don't belong on these premises.
Everyone feels like a nemesis.
You are my indigo reverie.
To whom do I fly in a hurry?

I know things can't get any better.
I'm the luckiest in town.
But, with you, I'll fit apter
Like monarchs and crowns
Life, for me, isn't about chores.
It is more about a living vision from the core.

You are my indigo reverie.
My soul's treasury

NEVER ENDING COMA

I feel like walking on a sharp-edged knife.

Resonating the sick, substandard strife
I can't handle this rife
Can't I escape this life?
Done with acting like a suitor for the best wife

Like your teacher said,
My leaves of desperation, devastation, happiness, and hope
May shed down on the heath
But I'm truly doted,
To the thought of being a happy family with little kids and
You, my only brace tree.
Rest all is mere trife.

On the very first track,
When you sing, "True beauty is true sadness",
I felt it in my bones.
In your words, it's in-**yun**,
The destiny that cascades love and faith one after another
To the heavens in an empty cobblestone
My love isn't just a trife

I would walk on a sharp-edged knife.
Breaking all the sick, substandard strife
I am not part of any rife
I will escape this life.
Done with acting like a suitor for the best wife

In my dusted-closed bookcase
In every novel, you are my vowel.
The never-ending coma,
You, my freedom key
My heart says, Just cut to the chase.
To you, my trail, a slow grovel
Leaving behind the trauma
My way through the sea

DON'T WAIT

I tried to break the jail bars.
I want to know what lies beneath these doors.
I try to break the subconscious lies.
I want to define my realm, but time flies.

I live a **still life**.
I think everybody does.
I can't explain it to myself
That the search for a reason never ends.
I don't have myself
Certainly not my happiness.
I can't live a framed life,
And follow the trends.

Keeping calm is always plaguing.
The fear of failing creeped in.
Adored by the alluring paintings
We feel excruciating sadness.

Am I living a still life?
I think everybody does.
I can't explain it to myself

My guilty admissions

Do I even have myself?

I lost the pride in my eyes.

I can't live a framed life

And follow the trends.

“Don’t wait for someone to be the one.”

“Rather wait for the only one.”

Someone wrote on a plane mirror.

That’s when I saw the frame’s rear

Don’t live the still life.

Like everyone does

The way to know life

Is feeling unworthy at midnights

All I have is myself.

I need nothing else.

I can't live a framed life

And follow the trends.

I'D DIE FOR YOU

It took an eternity to grab in, "What life truly is?"
The infinity, the ups, downs, smiles, and frowns
To endear the insanity beneath love, its bliss
Its petty, the hearts, flowers, hugs and kisses

Waiting for true love
Nothing feels above
Waiting for a white dove
Tear and rewove

Why do I forget the need to be loved?
I'm unloved.
You are held behoved.
Dear beloved

All day, I love you.
In my head
I see nothing coming ahead.
All day, I haven't seen you.
Left unread
Like I've always been dead.

We shall escape the city with a flying notice.
Losing inanity, the mess, stress, crux, and crisis
We shall define affinity, love, and providence.
Your virility and my femininity, Criss and Cross

Waiting for true love
Nothing feels above
Waiting for a white dove
Tear and rewove

I don't know you.
I never said hello to you.
I only feel you.
I never stood under snow with you.

Honey, I bleed red.
All day, I'd die for you.
I would shed
In my inapt bed

GREEN GRASS

I think of you standing there,
Confused "Who is this whiskey bottle for?"
Someone says, from afar,
"You bought it for yourself from the bar."

I think of you, forgetting the plans.
And promises made to your friends
The way you shrink your eyes,
And say sorry, with your hands up in defense.

You shall be **forgetful** of yesterday,
You shall be forgetful of today,
It isn't memory dearth,
Just lay on the green grass.

You carry a lot on your shoulders.
Every minute and every second, we grow older.
Don't take it harder.
My dear soldier

I have a lot left undone.
But honestly, I regret none.

Not hitting a home run

Fresh minds are fun.

I think of you, walking through the thorns.

Leaving yourself at home

How much have you borne?

It takes a lot to never be wrong.

It's alright to forget and cry.

It's alright to let things pass by.

You shall be forgetful of yesterday,

You shall be forgetful of today,

It isn’t memory dearth,

Just lay on the green grass.

OATHS AND OASIS

My reality has become a nightmare.
Will we ever get **closer**?
I see myself walking away from the dream door.
A beggar could never be a chooser.

I cement all gaps with allies.
Wielding with mere gold and silver, nothing but lies
I'm tired of the race and prizes.
I just want to die gazing into your eyes.

Is it wrong to want more?
Or escape a hard hour.
You and I shouldn't just be folklore.
But the moon and Venus from the night before

My words aren't wise.
Because I fail in black and white, if I strategize
But slowly, I realized
I belong on the edge of the sky.

"Stay there", gawking at the moon phases.
"Stay there", waiting for the arrival of Venus.

"Stay there", forgetting all the oaths.
"Stay there", probing the wounded oasis

I need the warmth in your glare.
I'm freezing to death right here.
All my delusions and ambitions fly in the air.
Do you even hear

I wonder how time flies.
And how much do I hold back and compromise.
Acting blind to all the lies
I've been living in paranoia with closed eyes.

"Stay there", gawking at the moon phases.
"Stay there", waiting for the arrival of Venus.
"Stay there", forgetting all the oaths.
"Stay there", probing the wounded oasis

RARITY

Dancing in the cold, pouring rain
Diamond ring, eye-piercing shine
Dining with pretty aged wine
I was quite sure I was crossing the line?

My ride has been disastrous.
I've always been this superfluous.
You've brought me down to verity
Why are you this infamous?
My dreams are risible and preposterous.

You are the only dream in my reality.
You are my only prayer and probity.
I've just realized all this is an absolute absurdity.
But still, shall we be a piece of rarity?

You called your past self a fool.
But you stood out of the pool.
Change is inevitable and also ghastful.
That led you to rule.

Always dreaming of an ideal

Far from what was there for me in real
I lived a life of love and credulity.
You sang your last words facing the ceil.
But the thought of "us" is surreal.

You are the only dream in my reality.
You are my only prayer and probity.
I've just realized all this is an absolute absurdity.
But still, shall we be a piece of rarity?

You made me want to dance in the cold rain.
And it made me love the tiny promise ring.
Love is no fantasy, but sharing pain
When you feel the same, just be my king.

ETHEREAL HOME

In different time zones, you'll never be alone.
Even on the darkest nights, you'll never be alone.
Even when you are the moon, you'll never be alone.
I'll be Venus beside you, glistening even if it's midday noon.

You've saved lives. I'm one in the pile.
We're under the same sky, yet you're **lonely**.
Scattered memories, a hotel room melancholy
We shall gather all of them in our minds and make a beautiful vinyl of our kind.
In the streets, buildings, and cities
We shall hopefully find our serenity.
I hope you find your ethereal home.

Ancient art and nature never filled the cleft left
Romance novels and old money never filled the cleft left.
Standing beside the seashore in silence didn't fill the cleft left.
My massive failure in finding our zone
It's my take on faith that you'll feel at home.

In the calmness of the narrow room, loud horns and commotion
The tangled fence you drew for yourself was set to be in liberation.

Rendezvous, Moulin Rouge, sunrise, and coffee session
I hope you find your ethereal home.

The truthfulness in your face, beyond the screens and cameras
It made me fall for the depth in your eyes that hopefully turns soft when it finds me.
Unlike the mythical characters and the deep blue sea, you're deeply sown.
I hope we find our ethereal home.

VIOLIN'S STRING

You throw a bouquet of flowers.
Lying flat on wild green grass
Gazing at the still, subtle sky
I lie in your muscled embrace.
Forgetting the world and the race
I descend in the look on your eye.

Sunrise, subtle breeze, and midday burn
Time-tripping from a violin string
In your eyes, I see them all sink in.
Violin's string has had the best win.
Twilight, shattered stars, and a full moon
Violin's string has got the best win.

Drowned in your eyes for hours
Getting a clear picture of Mars
Epitome of happiness, I'd gladly die
Healing all our burns and scars
Serenity will all be ours.
Time chooses to wait for us, and not fly.

Between the sun and the full moon

Time-tripping from a violin string
Your constant hunt for a reason
Violin's string has had the best win.
Amidst the chasing, our romantic heaven
Violin’s string has got the best win.

We shall be poetic.
Time tries to be frenetic.
But we’ll take it slow.
Just with the flow
Days will still be **hectic**.
Rushing makes it more pathetic.
Reason, we will know
We have to try hard, though.

I’m right here; why abstain?
Time-tripping from a violin string
Bound to share all the pain
Violin's string has had the best win.
We are our reason for being bornin’.
I’m right here; why abstain?
Bound to share all the pain
Violin’s string has got the best win.

EUGENE

Eternity on an open land
Who doesn't know he is saddened?
Thirst for the flame
He says he's got no name.

Dear Eugene,
I've always hankered to see the lanterns.
Dear wild flower,
You leave a sweet scar,
And the flower work burns.

Eternity in a flower field
Forever, I'll stay in the barren field.
For your return someday
My tiny footsteps on your way.

Dear Eugene,
I've always hankered to see the lanterns.
My wild flower,
You've left a sweet scar,
And the flower work burns.

“Please take the desire away from me”,
It scatters across the sky.
You weren’t just happy; it's also a memory.
Nothing was a lie.

I’m easily drawn.
To my dear moon:
If you haven’t shown
I wouldn’t have known.
The light of dawn
And the delight in its warmth.

When your inner self is devoured by your reverie
You know that we will fly.
If it's love and not us, I wouldn’t plea
I’d rather die.

I’m easily drawn.
To my dear moon:
If you haven’t shown,
I wouldn’t have known.
The light of dawn
And the delight in its warmth

Dear Eugene,

I've always hankered to see the lanterns.

My wild flower,

You leave a sweet scar,

And the flower work burns.

ROUSE OF CHAPTER NO.2

I try hard not to look back.
An attempt to follow your words
Just one call, and I'd shack
I fly around, like spring birds.

I take cold showers on rainy days.
I play loud music and ruminate.
I write letters in a dark room.
Is it the rouse of Chapter No. 2?

I listen to all the math classes.
I realize I'm delicate.
I walk fast under the full moon.
Is it the rouse of Chapter No. 2?

Have I really done my best?
Remaining life feels like a burden.
Have I really survived the worst?
The head feels like it's inside the lion's den.

I can't put up with the trends.
I believe "now is never late."

I act like a Roman in Rome.
Is it the rouse of Chapter No. 2?

I fake it for family and friends.
I have too much on my plate.
I lock myself in a small room.
Is it the rouse of Chapter No. 2?

I'm dying as an ailing lover.
To escape this sickness, I need your cure.
With no hope, I rest now.
Love prevails; prove me how.

Uncertain for years, I hover
Looking in the mirror, I said "Burn her".
Bleeding tears on my pillow
Is my faith facile and shallow?

"This woman was mad",
"She was dead."
It keeps being coined again and again.
"It was tough", I can't bargain.

I don't want you to be sad.

I wish you to be nothing but glad.
I would take all the pain.
With what you've left, an indigo stain.

I act fine and cry in silence.
I want to escape this gate.
My scream echoes in a dome.
Will there be a Chapter No. 2?

To my honest conscience
This is a long wait.
Will this love ever bloom?
Will there be a Chapter No. 2?

Will this love ever bloom?
Will there be Chapter No. 2?

IN SEARCH OF HUE, YOU

A year ago, it was this exact same train
Where all my travail and toil went in vain.
It was a sour, dour, and somber genesis
Of the bleakest chapters of my existence.
The yellow carnations they gave me
Inside out, wholly, it crushed me.

Whatever I see is always black and white
The reverie they designed for me is very bright.
I could never visibly see any intense color
I mistook yellow for orange; their spiel was blur.
I'm to blame. I broke the bubble of trust.
Solely blameworthy for the burst

Trying, bending, cracking, but breaking in the very end
I was too shattered to take in all the love, but I could pretend.
I couldn't keep mending all the broken pieces of me again
It is immaturity that comes with age. The perks are pain.

All they did was build an empire filled with color
I needed someone to save me. I wish I had a brother.
I loved the castle but can't continue to pluck basils.

I didn't know where I lacked; I wish I could also dazzle.
They are my light. I think about it on this train journey.
There was no wind on my face. I learnt, I can't buy it with money.

Sapphires, diamonds, and emeralds in weights of carats
Their colossal name and crown are too massive to inherit.
Abundance of brightness, working with vision for hue
Still struggling with an unpolarized image, I knew I lacked you.

I thought you were the shining golden moon up above.
Just like fireworks, a luminous treat for the eyes in love
But you lie on the grassland, loving nature as your own art.
Though you say we are under the same sky,
I wonder if we are beneath the same sky.

The beautiful bouquet of white carnations, I held
And I stood there under the midnight sky, and still sea
It made me feel claustrophobic and dead.

Can you please take the hint and reach out with flowers?
I can't fight this battle within myself now.
I need the hue that you have.
I'm waiting in the street.
Shredding a frozen teardrop

I’ve been waiting for a real long time.

www.ingramcontent.com/pod-product-compliance
Lightning Source LLC
LaVergne TN
LVHW041126150826
845673LV00007B/2187